The TRAGEDY of MACBETH

FAMILIUS

FAMILIUS

Published by Familius LLC, www.familius.com
Familius books are available at special discounts for bulk
purchases for sales promotions or for family or corporate use.
Special editions, including personalized covers, excerpts of
existing books, or books with corporate logos, can be created in
large quantities for special needs. For more information, contact
Premium Sales at 559-876-2170 or email specialmarkets@
familius.com.

Originally published by Sweet Cherry Publishing, Ltd, 2013
Text & illustration by Macaw Books, 2013

Library of Congress Catalog-in-Publication Data
2015942869
ISBN 9781942934288

Printed in the United States of America

Edited by Brooke Jorden
Cover design by David Miles

10 9 8 7 6 5 4 3 2 1

First Edition

About SHAKESPEARE

William Shakespeare, regarded as the greatest writer in the English language, was born in Stratford-upon-Avon in Warwickshire, England (around April 23, 1564). He was the third of eight children born to John and Mary Shakespeare.

Shakespeare was a poet, playwright, and dramatist. He is often known as England's national poet and the "Bard of Avon." Thirty-eight plays, 154 sonnets, two long narrative poems, and several other poems are attributed to him. Shakespeare's plays have been translated into every major language and are performed more often than those of any other playwright.

MAIN CHARACTERS

Macbeth is a Scottish general and the Thane of Glamis. Macbeth commits murder after murder once the prophecy of the three witches—that he would become the Thane of Cawdor—comes true. He is a brave soldier and powerful, but easily tempted.

Lady Macbeth is a deeply ambitious
woman who will stop at nothing
to have power and position. At the
beginning of the story, she is ruthless,
but later she is driven to insanity
and becomes a victim to her guilt.

The Three Witches are three mysterious hags who plot mischief against Macbeth by using their spells and prophecies. Their prediction prompts Macbeth to commit murders.

Macduff is a Scottish nobleman who is hostile toward Macbeth's rule. He seeks revenge against Macbeth for murdering his wife and child.

THE TRAGEDY OF MACBETH

During the reign of the great King Duncan of Scotland, there lived a brave and gallant thane (lord) called Macbeth. He was one of the

king's most trusted servants and was his most loyal and successful general during war. Macbeth led the Scottish troops to victory at every turn, vanquishing large and powerful armies and never showing any fear.

Very recently, the reign of King Duncan had faced a

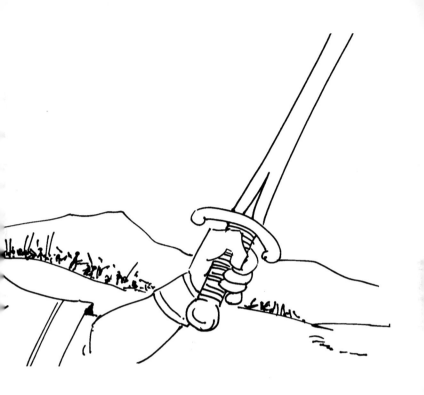

threat from a rebel, the Thane
of Cawdor, assisted by the
troops of the king of Norway,
Scotland's enemy. No match
for Macbeth's swordsmanship
and bravery, the rebel army
was completely routed and the
Scottish army was left victorious.

Now, the story of Macbeth

begins from the time of this war. He was returning from the battlefield with his friend, the noble Banquo, when suddenly they were approached by three very haggard-looking witches. Withered and unearthly, they

looked like the
walking dead. These
witches raised their
bony fingers to
their skinny lips and
motioned the men to stop. Then
the first one turned to them and

said, "All hail Macbeth, Thane of Glamis!" Macbeth was not surprised to hear this as he was, indeed, the Thane of Glamis, but what came next shocked both Macbeth and Banquo.

The second witch said, "All hail Macbeth, Thane of Cawdor." And before Macbeth could react,

the third witch came forth and exclaimed, "All hail Macbeth, who shall be king hereafter!"

"Stay, you imperfect speakers, tell me more!" Macbeth cried, but the three witches vanished into thin air without another word.

Macbeth and Banquo were still wondering in disbelief when they were met on the road by some of King Duncan's soldiers.

After greeting one another,
the soldiers informed Macbeth
that since the Thane of Cawdor
had betrayed King Duncan
and led his armies against him,
the king had declared that he
would be hanged for treason. He
also told the duo that Duncan

had named Macbeth the new
Thane of Cawdor as a reward
for his gallant and loyal services
to the throne over the years.

Macbeth and Banquo
could not believe what they
were hearing. It had been just
minutes since the second witch

predicted that Macbeth would be appointed the Thane of Cawdor. Could it be true?

Macbeth started to wonder if the witches could really have seen the future! *Two truths were told. If the first prediction came true, I*

might become king, too. Still, the
prospect seemed too far-fetched,
so Macbeth concluded
that if fate would
have him be king,
it would happen,
and there was

nothing he could do about it. He decided not to worry himself any further, come what may. He was, of course, elated at being appointed the Thane of Cawdor and thanked the messengers for bringing him such delightful news.

That evening, when Macbeth met Duncan, the great King of Scotland, he invited him to spend a day with him in his castle. Duncan

readily consented. Now Macbeth
needed to get his castle in order
for the king's arrival, so he
wrote a letter to his wife, Lady
Macbeth, and told her about
the plan. While writing, he also
mentioned the three witches and
their odd prophecies, adding
how one of those prophecies

had already come true.

When Lady Macbeth read the letter, her mind started racing, and she could think of nothing else. Her husband was now no longer just the Thane of Glamis but also the Thane of Cawdor, as per the prophecy. Lady Macbeth was therefore convinced that

her husband would soon be the
new King of Scotland, if he had
the ambition to make it so.

Her plan was simple.
Since Duncan was coming
to their castle that evening,
all they would have to do was
kill him and then the witches'

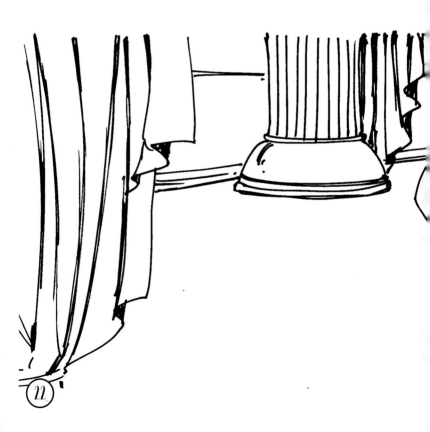

second prophecy would also come true. If Macbeth was destined to be king, Duncan had to die that night.

When Macbeth returned to his castle, Lady Macbeth confided in him about her sinister plan. At first, Macbeth rejected idea of killing the king. Duncan had

always been a fair and wise ruler,
and as his subject and his host,
Macbeth felt it was his duty to
defend him and keep him safe.

But Lady Macbeth knew
her husband well and
asked, "Are you afraid?"

Not one to be
called a coward,

Macbeth protested, "I dare do all that may become a man! But what if we should fail?"

"Gather your courage, and we will not fail. Leave all the rest to me," Lady Macbeth assured him.

They agreed that Lady Macbeth would ring her bell at the moment he should kill the

king. That night, as Macbeth
waited in King Duncan's
chambers for his wife's signal, he
suddenly saw a dagger dangling
before him in the air. With

amazement, he said, "Is this a dagger that I see before me, the handle toward my hand?" He tried to grab it from the air, but his hand passed right through the vision, and he began to wonder if it was only a dream. "Are you a dagger of the

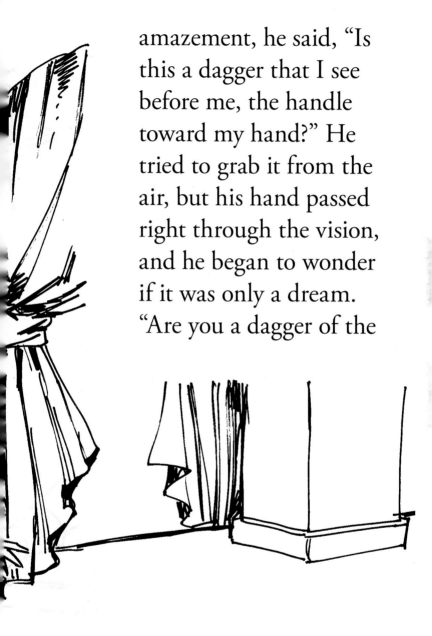

mind, a false creation, proceeding from the heat-oppressed brain?" Unable to bear his anxiety any longer, he heard the sound of a bell chiming—his wife's signal. Macbeth raised the dagger over the king, saying, "The bell invites me. Hear it not, Duncan, for it is a knell that summons you to heaven or to hell." So saying, Macbeth murdered his own king.

While Lady Macbeth waited for Macbeth's return, she

grew restless, scared that her husband might get caught in the act or that he would lose his nerve and not be able to go through with their muderous plan. However, her fears were put to rest when Macbeth returned

with blood on his hands.

The couple soon retired to their rooms, where Macbeth washed the blood from his hands and pretended to be asleep. Soon it was morning and the king's guards arrived to rouse Duncan.

When they realized that the
king had been murdered, they
immediately raised the alarm:
"Awake, awake! Ring the alarm-
bell! Murder and treason!"

Macbeth, on hearing the
news, pretended to be enraged.
With a cry, he ran into the
room and killed the two guards

before they could deny their involvement in the king's death. The guards appeared to be guilty, so no one suspected that Macbeth was involved.

Prince Malcolm and Prince Donalbain, the king's sons, hurried out of their rooms when they heard the commotion.

They realized that they might
be the next targets of the vicious
murderer, so the two princes
decided to run away from
Scotland at once—Malcolm
would flee to England, while
Donalbain would rush to Ireland,
where they would both be safe.

With the rightful heirs to the crown missing, Macbeth was anointed the new King of Scotland. The second prophecy of the witches had come true.

Macbeth at once settled into his new kingly duties. But he still had one thought nagging at the back of his mind—he was afraid that Banquo, his close friend of many years, would suspect something was amiss. After all, Banquo was the only other witness to the witches' prophecies, and he might come

to the conclusion that the murderer was none other than Macbeth. Therefore, he decided to have Banquo killed.

One night, Macbeth arranged a banquet for his aides and ministers. Banquo, along with his son, Fleance, was supposed to attend, but alas,

Macbeth had other plans for
him. As Banquo set off, three
men came out of the bushes and
stabbed him. They tried to grab
Fleance as well, but Fleance's
horse, seeing the attackers
approach, galloped off into the
darkness and Fleance was saved.

That evening, when the
banquet began, Macbeth's guilt

made him start hallucinating.
He believed he saw Banquo's
ghost enter the room and sit at
Macbeth's place at the table.

When asked to sit and join the others, Macbeth could not. In his mind, the table was full.

Speaking to an empty chair, Macbeth kept saying, "You cannot say I did it. Never shake your gory locks at me."

No one else could
see the ghost, so
they believed
their king must
be unwell.

Lady Macbeth, realizing that
her husband was in a
state of delirium, was
scared that he might say
more than he should.
She immediately told
all those gathered there
that he was unwell and
asked them to leave.

Later, when
Macbeth had regained
his sanity, he told his
wife that he would have
to pay the three witches

another visit. He had to know what else lay in store for him.

The next day, he retraced his steps along the same path he had taken the first time he met the witches. He found them gathered around a large boiling pot and asked them to tell him what

45

his future would hold. The first
witch chanted, "Double, double,
toil and trouble. Fire burn and
cauldron bubble." When she
finished her spell, a frightening
face appeared in the steam rising
from the pot. The image said,
"Macbeth! Macbeth! Macbeth!
Beware Macduff!" As soon as the

first image was gone, another face appeared, who said, "Be bloody, bold, and resolute; laugh to scorn the power of man, for none of woman born shall harm Macbeth." Finally, a third apparition appeared and informed him,

"Macbeth shall never be vanquished until the great Birnam Woods begin to walk against him."

Macbeth was relieved. Since every man has a mother and trees couldn't possibly uproot themselves and start to walk, he assumed that he could never be killed.

Still, Macbeth did not want to take any chances, so he sent some of his hired murderers to Macduff's castle to kill him. When they arrived, they found that Macduff had already left for England. In his absence,

the murderers killed everyone
in the castle, including
Macduff's wife and children.

Meanwhile, Prince Malcolm
and Macduff were in England,
talking about the affairs in
Scotland. Malcolm assured his

friend that the English royalty had been very helpful and had provided him with a battery of ten thousand fine soldiers. He told Macduff that there would soon be an attack on Scotland to steal the throne away from

Macbeth. While they were finalizing the plans, a Scottish nobleman, Ross, arrived. He had just come back from Scotland with terrible news. He told

Macduff about the deaths
of his wife and children.

Macduff was shocked and
heartbroken at the news, but
his sorrow soon turned to
anger, and he swore that he
would return to Scotland and
take his revenge against the
perpetrator of this crime.

While Macduff planned to
wage a war against Scotland,
a most unusual thing was
happening in the Macbeth's
palace in Scotland. The queen's
maid had ordered the doctor to

come that night, as there was a
rather strange thing happening
that he needed to see for himself.
They waited for quite some time
after everyone had gone to sleep.
Then, suddenly, they heard a
door open and the light from a
candle filled the room. It was

the queen. It seemed that she
was sleepwalking or in some sort
of trance. She was
trying to scrub her
hands and kept
saying, "Out,
damned spot!
Out, I say!" She

kept mumbling about blood and the murder of the king and Macduff's wife. Finally, she exclaimed, "Will these hands never be clean? Here's the smell of the blood still. All the perfumes of Arabia will not sweeten this little hand." Then, as mysteriously as she had arrived,

she left. Clearly, her guilt was driving her mad.

The next day, the whole of Scotland was filled with the news that the English army had arrived, led by Prince Malcolm and Macduff. Macbeth immediately issued orders to keep

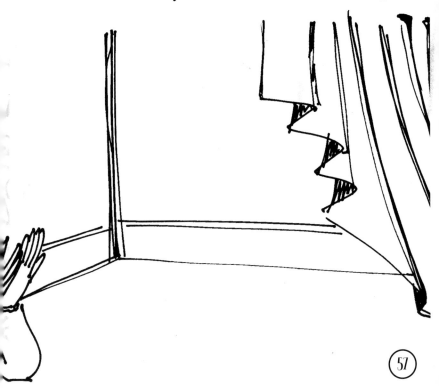

a watch on their movements and even brought the army out to defend the castle at Dunsinane Hill in the event of an attack.

While the Scottish army prepared to fight, the English army camped at Birnam Woods. Prince Malcolm instructed his men to break some branches off the trees and tie them to their bodies before laying siege

to the castle. That way, their
numbers would be misleading.

A soldier reported to Macbeth
that the trees appeared to be
approaching the castle. Macbeth
immediately remembered the
warning he had received from the
third apparition in the presence
of the three witches. He had
been warned that he would rule
until the great Birnam Woods
walked toward Dunsinane Hill.

As he was contemplating his

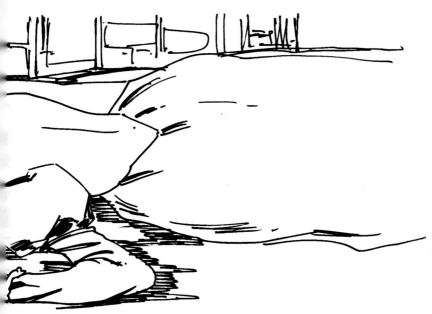

next course of action, a cry rang
through the palace walls. Lady
Macbeth, overcome by guilt, had
jumped from the roof and killed
herself. Mourning his
wife and knowing that
his own time was
coming to an end,
Macbeth cried, "Out,
out, brief candle!
Life's but a walking

shadow, a poor player that struts and frets his hour upon the stage and then is heard no more."

Macbeth decided to put on his armor and leave the castle alone.

As he walked through

the forest, he was confronted by Macduff, ready to avenge the murder of his family. Their swords clashed, but neither man could gain any advantage.

Macbeth boasted of what the third apparition had told him, that no man born of a woman could kill him, and that Macduff was wasting his time. To this, Macduff replied, "Then let me tell you that from my mother's womb I was untimely taken by the doctor. I was not born of a woman, but delivered by a man."

Now Macbeth knew his time had come. With a flash and clash of steel, Macbeth lay defeated at the feet of the valiant Macduff. All the prophecies had come true, and the evil era of Macbeth was over.

Prince Malcolm regained the throne that was rightfully his after the death of his father. Under his reign, Scotland once again rose to its past state of glory.

$6.95 US
Children

When three meddlesome witches issue a prophecy that Macbeth will become king, he and his ambitious wife will stop at nothing to make it come true—even murder. But can they enjoy their success, or will guilt and paranoia drive them mad?

Set in medieval Scotland, *The Tragedy of Macbeth* is one of Shakespeare's darkest plays. Some even claim the play itself is haunted. When performing this tragedy, superstitious actors refuse to say the name of the play aloud, fearing a dark curse will haunt them if they do. Instead, they call it "The Scottish Play" and keep a keen eye out for ghosts and witches.

WILLIAM SHAKESPEARE (1564-1616)

Playwright. Poet. Actor. Producer. Legend. William Shakespeare is widely regarded as one of the greatest writers in the English language, and his work has influenced centuries of writers and thinkers. His collected works—from plays to poems—have been translated into every language and are performed to the delight of audiences the world over.

ISBN 978-1-942934-28-8

5 0 6 9 5 >

9 781942 934288

FAMILIUS

HELPING FAMILIES BE HAPPY

Visit us at www.familius.com for books, articles, and videos to help your family be happy.